Peer Coaching
Made Simple

Other books
by Dennis E. Coates, Ph.D.

For organizations:

Connect with Your Team: Mastering the Top 10 Communication Skills (with Meredith M. Bell)

The Dark Secret of HRD: Four Things You Need to Know to Stop Wasting Money on Training

For parents:

How Your Teen Can Grow a Smarter Brain

Connect with Your Kid

Conversations with the Wise Uncle

Conversations with the Wise Aunt (with Kathleen Scott)

Preparing Your Teen for Life

The Sacred Purpose

Poetry:

To the Colors (with Mark Hamilton)

Peer Coaching Made Simple

*How to Do the 6 Things
That Matter Most
When Helping Someone Improve a Skill*

Dennis E. Coates, Ph.D.

First Summit Publishing

Peer Coaching Made Simple: How to Do the 6 Things That Matter Most When Helping Someone Improve a Skill

Printed in the United States of America

First Summit Publishing
An imprint of Performance Support Systems, Inc.
757-873-3700

Cover and book design: Paula Schlauch

ISBN: 978-1-7348051-4-7

For caring people everywhere
who are committed to
other people's success

"Knowing is not enough;

we must apply.

Willing is not enough;

we must do."

—Bruce Lee

Contents

So Someone Asked You to Be Their Peer Coach

If you've never done this before, at first the idea of being a peer coach might sound a little scary. Actually, all you'll be doing is giving support to someone while they work on skills to be more effective as they do their job. As you read this brief book, you're going to find out that you already know how to do most of what's needed. It's a little like leading a meeting or being a good friend. So there's no need to be nervous about it.

As you read each chapter, notice how simple it is to be a peer coach and tell yourself: *I can do that.*

You don't need to be intimidated by the idea of being somebody's coach.

Yes, many people make coaching their profession: executive coaches, business coaches, parent coaches, life coaches, athletic coaches, trainers, counselors, consultants, therapists, and others. For sure, they've had plenty of education and training to prepare them for these careers.

But the idea that people can coach each other while they're trying to be more effective is not revolutionary. For example, experienced school teachers have always done this to help others who are new to the profession. And moms have been getting together to share their know-how with each other for...well, forever.

Today, we call this helping activity "peer coaching." Coaching someone who is working to improve a skill is more like being a friend or a mentor. You do it because you care about someone else's success. Very likely the person who needs your help is someone you know well, such as a friend or a coworker.

The purpose of this book is to give you a few ideas to make your coaching interactions more effective.

To illustrate my suggestions, I've included sample dialogues. I've chosen workplace examples, because peer coaching is a familiar practice in organizations. I believe you can relate to these illustrations, whether you're an employee in a business, a school teacher, or a parent helping another parent.

The examples describe someone who is working on the skills that are the topic of the book, *Connect with Your Team: Mastering the Top 10 Communication Skills.* The book is a guide for improving what I've learned are the most important workplace communication skills.

A typical coaching process involves meeting regularly with the person you're coaching, reviewing what they committed to do in real-world situations, and talking about what they learned from these experiences. At the end of the meeting, you ask the person to set new action goals to accomplish before the next meeting.

Your coaching is extremely helpful because reading books or attending courses is only the beginning. Once someone learns what they should be doing, they need to make the skill their habitual response in relationships. Realistically, replacing an old habit with a new skill takes time. It's like getting better at anything—it takes practice, practice, and more practice. It takes a lot of "reps" to stimulate the brain to rewire itself. Only then will a person be comfortable responding automatically with an improved skill.

Along the way, this self-development effort can sometimes be frustrating. Someone might forget to apply the skill, or their initial attempts might feel awkward and ineffective. Even with good intentions and motivation, after a while a person can get discouraged.

This is why it helps to have a coach.

To stay on track and master a skill, people benefit from having accountability, reminders, and encouragement. Very likely, this is why someone has asked you to be their peer coach.

It's easier than you think to help someone get stronger as a contributor to team results.

It Really Is Simple...
The 6 Basics of
Peer Coaching

To be a helpful peer coach, you don't need special training. All you need is the desire to be supportive and the willingness to put into practice some of the tips in this book. To boost your confidence, this brief guide will suggest ways to use skills you probably already have, such as holding someone accountable, listening, asking questions that get someone to think, and giving encouragement.

The person you're coaching may ask for your opinions, ideas, and help setting goals. As you interact with someone you're coaching, you may find it useful to refer to this book as you prepare to meet with them. Like the person you're helping, the more you apply the guidance here, the more confident and helpful you'll become.

If the person you're coaching is trying to improve the way they interact with others, they may be using the book, *Connect with*

Your Team. If so, I encourage you to get your own copy, so you're familiar with the skills they're working on.

As you meet with someone to help them on their development journey, appreciate that it will take time for them to make a new skill a habit. They'll need to persist as they continue to apply it on the job and learn from their successes and frustrations. You can help them stay positive and focused.

Also, because it's challenging to replace an old habit with a more useful one, they'll need to work on one skill at a time. You can help them stay focused. With your support, after several weeks they may become more comfortable with the new way of connecting. At that point, they may decide to work on another skill.

This book explains in six chapters how you can help someone stay on track to improve the way they interact with others:

1. **ACCOUNTABILITY**: *How a Peer Coach Inspires Motivation*

2. *A Peer Coach's Superpower:* **LISTENING**

3. *Giving Advice...***WHAT TO DO INSTEAD**

4. **LEARNING FROM EXPERIENCE**...*the Foundation of Skill-Building*

5. **FEEDBACK** *That Feels Good*

6. **ENCOURAGEMENT** *That Energizes*

As you read, think about how you can use these six tips to be an effective peer coach.

ACCOUNTABILITY: How a Peer Coach Inspires Motivation

Replacing an old work habit with a new skill isn't easy, because it involves going against the grain of the established habit. An old habit is a pattern of behavior that is driven by circuits in the brain, which were created by countless repetitions of the behavior over the years. To replace it with a new skill, people need to rewire their brains. This means lots of repetitions of the new behavior over time.

This can be challenging, because before a new skill is established, the old habit can kick in, or people can make mistakes and get discouraged. The danger is that they'll give up before they ingrain the new skill. As their coach, you can help keep them positive and on track.

Holding the person you're coaching accountable can be powerful, because knowing you'll be checking on them gives them another reason to do the hard things while making a change. They

Knowing that someone will be checking their progress can motivate them to do the work.

know *you* know what they said they will do, and they know you'll ask them about it.

It's kind of like losing weight. If someone doesn't stand on the scale each week to check progress, it could be all too easy to let things slide. With the scale, you can tell whether you're actually moving forward. This form of accountability is a key element of the best weight loss programs. It inspires and motivates people to do what they said they would do until they get results.

Here's how to set up accountability:

1. When someone approaches you to be their peer coach, settle on how and when you'll make contact. Face-to-face? Phone? Email? Online? Twice a week? Monthly?

2. In your initial meeting, learn what kind of self-development they want to work on. You can help them focus by encouraging them to work on improving one skill at a time—the skill they'll be working on for the next several weeks.

3. Then find out what they want to do to work on the skill before the next meeting. Ask them what specific on-the-job actions they'll commit to before the next meeting—exactly what, when, where, with whom, how much, and so on.

4. Keep a record of these commitments.

5. And then, the next time you meet with them, ask them what they did—how each of these actions worked for them.

6. Before you conclude your coaching session, help them reset their goal with another series of actions to accomplish before the next meeting.

Rashid sets Alfredo
up to be accountable....

Rashid has agreed to be Alfredo's peer coach. Here's how the first meeting went...

Rashid: "So I'm going to be your peer coach!"

Alfredo: "Cool. Have you ever done this before?"

Rashid: "No. But Mack and Myla gave me some tips. What are you trying to do?"

Alfredo: "I'm just getting started. I've been reading the book, *Connect with Your Team*. It recommends starting with listening skills, so I guess that's what I'll do."

Rashid: "Great. I have that book, too. I'll bookmark the listening chapter. Have you read that chapter yet?"

Alfredo: "Yup."

Rashid: "Me, too. My understanding is that listening is actually several skills rolled into one. Is there one aspect you'd like to focus on first?"

Alfredo: "I like the bit about expressing empathy. I thought that was cool. I never thought of expressing empathy as a skill before, something you could get good at. So maybe I can start with that."

Rashid: "Sure. Do you want to keep meeting on Zoom?"

Alfredo: "Fine with me."

Rashid: "Once a week okay with you?"

Alfredo: "I think every other week would be better. Give me some time to work on it."

Rashid: "Good. Every other week. What day and time are best for you?"

Alfredo: "How about we start first thing in the morning on Monday, every other Monday. Say nine o'clock?"

Rashid: "Done. So a week from Monday we'll meet again. I'll contact you."

Alfredo: "Great."

Rashid: "So Alfredo, what will you do during the next couple weeks to work on empathy?"

Alfredo: "I'll try do what the book says. I'll work on doing that."

Rashid: "That's fine. But I think the way this works is you commit to specific actions, and then we talk about what you did at the next meeting. As your peer coach, I'd like to hear what you will do, with whom, how often, that sort of thing. I'll help you be accountable."

Alfredo: "Okay."

Rashid: "So specifically, what do you commit to doing about improving the way you express empathy?"

Alfredo: "Hmm. Well, I plan to follow the book's instructions. Here's what I'm thinking. As I work with my group, I'll be on the lookout for instances when someone is expressing some kind of emotion. I'll respond with a statement of empathy and see how it goes."

Rashid: "What's your goal? Do this once? Twice? Four times?"

Alfredo: "I'll shoot for trying this five times during the coming two weeks. How's that?"

Rashid: "Great! And then we'll talk about how it went for you."

Alfredo: "Sounds good. I think that will help."

Rashid: "All right! I'm looking forward to hearing about it."

IN SUMMARY...

This was Rashid's first meeting with Alfredo, so it was brief. He encouraged Alfredo to set some very specific action goals, so he could get him to talk about them at their next meeting. Two weeks later, they met again on Zoom and talked about what happened. Alfredo had tried the empathy techniques with five different people and got a mixture of reactions. He and Rashid talked about why people reacted the way they did and what Alfredo could learn from each instance. Rashid discovered that being a peer coach felt natural to him, and Alfredo felt that talking with a coach actually helped him improve. A few months later, he was still working on empathy, and Rashid was still enjoying these peer coaching meetings.

A Peer Coach's
Superpower:
LISTENING

In your coaching role, you'll often be involved in conversation.

But you should expect that most of the time, you'll need to be *listening* instead, which is a different skill.

Most people don't think about how they listen, so they don't make a special effort to listen well. They believe it's just something you naturally do in conversation. When people talk, you listen. When you talk, they listen.

The point of listening well is to avoid misunderstanding what the other person is trying to express.

This can be easier said than done. The spoken word is never as easy to make sense of as the written word. When writing, people get to revise their message until they're sure it says what they want it to say. The person you're coaching won't get to do that. Like most people, they may start with some small talk before launching into accounts of their experiences. Along the way, they might express opinions, ideas, and feelings.

All this could be revealing. But the person you're coaching may think differently than you do. There may be differences in education, skills, experience, needs, goals, values, personality—and more. They may communicate in a way that's not familiar to you. In their efforts to express themselves, they may jump back and forth in time, making it hard for you to understand the sequence of events. They might get to the point quickly, or they might digress.

The bottom line is that the person speaking to you may not make it easy for you to understand the points they're trying to make. If you're not focused on listening well, you could misunderstand what you hear. What you think they said may not be what they meant. And there may be important things you don't hear because they're reluctant to tell you about them.

With all this going on, you'll need to be the best listener you can be, just to understand what people are trying to say.

The Keys to Turning On Your Listening Superpower

Here's how you can make sure you actually "get the message."

1. Recognize when it's time to listen

Be aware when the person you're coaching is about to tell you something about their learning. In other words, know when it's time to *stop conversing* and *start listening*.

2. Focus your attention

When listening, don't do anything else. Don't multi-task or let anything distract you—not even your thoughts. Let the other person do most of the talking. Listening is mostly about being quiet and focusing on them. It's not about telling your own stories, giving your own opinions, laying out your reasoning, offering your ideas, or giving advice. Your brain needs to be focused on making sense of what the person is trying to say. Even if your knowledge, experience and wisdom kick in and you feel a powerful impulse to give your two cents, don't do it. And be careful not to interrupt. Interrupting is a tell-tale sign that you aren't listening. So while they're talking, make the speaker feel like the most important person in your world.

3. Listen for the meaning

Think about what the person is saying and how they're saying it in order to understand *why* they're saying it— the point they're trying to make. Make an effort to pick up on both verbal and nonverbal messages. Consider their tone of voice, facial expressions, gestures, and other body language. If they're sharing their feelings, express empathy.

4. Check the meaning

When you think you understand some of what the speaker has said, don't assume you got it right. To be sure, tell the speaker—in your own words—what you think you've understood so far:

- "You seem to be saying that...."
- "Do you mean...."
- "It sounds like...."
- "So you...."
- "You feel that...."
- "Do I understand that...."

5. *Ask for more information*

The speaker will let you know whether you got it right. Either way, encourage the person to continue, so you can listen for more meaning and check again. Continue checking until you're sure you've understood the whole message.

As you can see from this way of listening, there's more to it than just paying attention. It's an active process in which you try to grasp the point the person's trying to make, while checking to be sure you've understood it correctly. If you listen this way, you'll know whether you "got the message." And the speaker will know it, too—which will be gratifying for both of you.

People love being heard.

Maria listens to Will....

Maria is Will's peer coach. During their weekly accountability meeting, she listened to Will's report...

Will: "Yesterday, I had a golden opportunity to give Chad feedback."

Maria: "Great! How did that go?"

Will: "I've been trying to be more specific about behavior."

Maria: "Right. How did it go?"

Will: "Well, Chad was late with his input again, so he was holding everything up. And I pointed that out to him."

Maria: "What did you say?"

Will: "I said something like, 'Chad, you're late again, and so our team report is being held up.'"

Maria: "How did he react to that?"

Will: "He had his usual excuses about being swamped."

Maria: "Then what?"

Will: "To be honest, I hate excuses. He's holding back the team. Everybody else managed to get their stuff to me on time."

Maria: "So how did you handle it?"

Will: "I told him I'd love it if he'd manage his time better."

Maria: "How did that go down?"

Will: "He got real defensive and angry and accused me of piling on more stuff than he could possibly deal with."

Maria: "How did you react to that?"

Will: "I told him everyone has a lot to do and they manage to get their input in, and I expect him to be on time next week."

Maria: "And...?"

Will: "He just walked off in a huff."

Maria: "So how do you feel about the way it went?"

Will: "It didn't play out the way I hoped. He didn't accept my feedback very well."

Maria: "Why do you think it didn't work so well?"

Will: "You know, I think I forgot to begin with a positive. I know you're supposed to do that. That's kind of new for me, and I sometimes forget to do that."

Maria: "You think you got off on the wrong foot, hitting him with a negative first."

Will: "Right."

Maria: "Sounds like you know how you want to handle it next time."

Will: "Yeah. I probably should review that chapter on feedback again."

Maria: "Chapter 10."

Will: "I think that's it."

Maria: "Sounds like a plan. Maybe this situation didn't go as well as you hoped, but my sense is that lately you've been having more success with this. You know it's a process, learning from things that don't go well. Like the book says, keep trying."

Will: "Right. Thanks for that. Let's talk again next Friday."

IN SUMMARY...

In this example, Maria encouraged Will to do most of the talking. Instead of giving advice, she listened to understand and encouraged him to continue explaining. She let him figure out what went wrong and what he learned from it.

The key: when talking with the person you're coaching, always be alert to opportunities to check what you think you're hearing. You can learn more about listening to understand in Chapter 4 of *Connect with Your Team*.

Well-intentioned people who want to help often feel the need to give advice. But when you're peer coaching, there's a better way. This is the topic of the next chapter.

Giving Advice... WHAT TO DO INSTEAD

There are problems with giving advice. For one thing, your suggestion may not be the best one for the person you're coaching. You weren't there to experience their situation, so you don't have all the facts. If they follow your advice and it doesn't work for them, you bear some responsibility for that. Also, giving advice doesn't give them credit for their ability to work through their own issues. If they make mistakes, learning from them is a valuable part of skill-building. And when they're successful, you don't want them to give you the credit; you want them to feel a sense of ownership and self-confidence.

So, if you feel the urge to offer a suggestion or an idea, what's a more helpful approach?

The answer: *ask open-ended questions to get them to think.*

> **When coaching, you may get an idea or think of a helpful solution.**
>
> **Resist the urge to give advice. Instead, encourage the other person to do their own thinking.**

In other words, don't ask questions that can be answered with a fact or a simple "yes" or "no." Questions that probe for facts can bring communication to a halt. For example, if they answer, "Yesterday about two-thirty," you have to get the interaction going again.

When the person you're coaching has finished making a point and you have confirmed that you understand, ask questions that encourage them to continue explaining what they're trying to say. Also, you may sense that they're faced with certain issues or challenges. Don't take ownership of them by offering your own ideas. Instead, encourage the speaker to think about possible solutions. Some examples:

- "Then what happened?"
- "How do you feel about that?"
- "Can you give me an example?"
- "What's your opinion?"
- "What have you tried?"

Nearly always, a person can reason through to solutions, so the best thing you can do is encourage them to do their own thinking. But on occasion, someone could be genuinely stumped. They may be at a total loss to know what to do, and they beg for your advice. In this case, you'll have to make a judgment call. While it may be helpful to share your experience, you need to be cautious. Qualify what you say with something like this: *"I'm not sure what your situation is like, but this has worked for me...."*

Lucas coaches Sheryl to think....

During Sheryl's weekly meeting with her peer coach, she wasn't happy about her progress...

Sheryl: "This hasn't been a good week. I'm so frustrated!"

Lucas: "Tell me about it."

Sheryl: "I honestly have too much on my plate. I get to working on something and Bob gives me another number one priority."

Lucas: "You must feel like you're falling behind."

Sheryl: "No kidding. I know we're supposed to talk about my efforts to be a better listener, but honestly I don't have anything to report."

Lucas: "You were so busy you didn't have any chances to listen."

Sheryl: "No, I think I had plenty of chances. I was just so rushed I didn't realize the opportunity was there until afterward, and it was too late."

Lucas: "It must be frustrating to know what you could be doing and not be able to recognize when to do it."

Sheryl: "I feel bad about it."

Lucas: "My sense is that it's not easy to change the way you listen, and that failures like this are kind of par for the course."

Sheryl: "That doesn't make me feel better."

Lucas: "What would you like to do about it?"

Sheryl: "I really need to get better at noticing these listening opportunities when they happen."

Lucas: "What can you do to make this happen?"

Sheryl: "I'm remembering what I read in that book about listening moments."

Lucas: "What about it?"

Sheryl: "It was about noticing when you need to be listening, that this is part of the skill."

Lucas: "So you're saying you want to focus on that."

Sheryl: "Yes. I probably need to reread that part and do a better job."

Lucas: "Chapter 4."

Sheryl: "Yeah."

Lucas: "Is this your goal for next week?"

Sheryl: "Yes. I'm going to get my radar turned on and start grabbing these moments."

IN SUMMARY...

While Lucas probably knew what Sheryl should to do, he avoided giving advice. Instead, he got Sheryl to think her way to a solution. This simple approach is about asking open-ended questions that encourage people to do their own reasoning, come to their own conclusions, solve their own problems, set their own goals, and make their own plans.

When peer coaching, be aware of any impulse to give advice. Remember that these are opportunities for the other person to do their own thinking. You can learn more about encouraging people to think for themselves in Chapter 5 of *Connect with Your Team*.

One of the most helpful kinds of thinking you can encourage is for someone to analyze something that happened so they learn from it. This is the topic of the next chapter.

LEARNING FROM EXPERIENCE...
the Foundation of Skill-Building

People don't always learn from what happens to them. It's possible to have dozens of experiences every day. But to capture the lessons, people have to consciously think about what happened and why. If they don't, it's possible not much will be learned, and they might repeat their mistakes.

Experience really is the best teacher. People can learn important lessons from what happens to them. But sometimes they don't.

Consciously learning from experience not only helps people get better at what they're doing, it accelerates their skill development. You can help the person you're coaching reflect by asking open-ended questions like these:

1. **What happened?** The details of an event need to be recalled in order to make sense of them. What was the sequence of events? What did you do? How did others react? How do you feel about it?

2. **Why did you handle it this way?** Things happen for a reason. To imagine a better way to handle a situation like this, try to understand why things occurred the way they did. What helped or hindered? What led to the outcome?

3. **What were the consequences?** Appreciating the impact of what happened creates the motivation to handle situations like this more effectively. Benefits? Costs? Problems? Resolutions?

4. **How would you handle a similar situation in the future?** What did you learn from this experience? What basic principles? How are you going to apply the lesson?

5. **What are your next steps?** What will you do going forward to implement this learning?

These questions have a logical sequence; but when coaching, the other person might begin connecting the dots without your help. They might even skip a step and jump to what they learned.

People aren't perfect, and it's hard to change a habit. Mistakes and failures can be steps toward growth. If they learn the lessons of experience and if they persist, the percentage of successes will increase. The key is to learn something from every success and every shortfall.

Mack helps Cece discover the lesson....

During a conversation between Cece and Mack, her peer coach, Cece described a recent encounter with her manager...

Cece: "On Wednesday, I really got into it with Iris."

Mack: "What happened?"

Cece: "I lost my cool."

Mack: "What do you mean?"

Cece: "She accused me of being disloyal."

Mack: "Why do you think she said that?"

Cece: "I don't know. I'm totally loyal to her and our group. Word got out about our plans somehow and it got back to her. She blamed me."

Mack: "How did you react to that?"

Cece: "I said some stuff I wish I could take back. I told her it wasn't my fault and maybe she did something that caused the leak."

Mack: "How did she react to that?"

Cece: "She got mad. She said I have a big mouth, that I talk too much. She said loose lips sink ships or something like that."

Mack: "What are you thinking about that?"

Cece: "Well, I'm not the leak. She said keep it under wraps until we go final, and that's what I did."

Mack: "Where do things stand now?"

Cece: "She thinks I'm not trustworthy."

Mack: "What could you have done to handle her accusation differently?"

Cece: "I probably should have tried to listen to her. But she took me by surprise, and it upset me. I felt attacked."

Mack: "What do you think would have happened if you had tried listening?"

Cece: "She was upset, and she blamed me. I don't know why. Maybe if I had tried listening, she would have offered an explanation."

Mack: "And that would have defused things?"

Cece: "Maybe. Instead of getting defensive and emotional, maybe we could have just talked about it."

Mack: "So listening might have prevented the blow-up."

Cece: "Probably. I really need help with listening. That's why you're coaching me!"

Mack: "So what's next?"

Cece: "I guess I need to go apologize. And then, regardless of what she says next, I'll practice my listening."

Mack: "Good luck. Let's talk again next week. I'd love to hear how this works for you."

Cece: "Thanks, coach!"

IN SUMMARY...

Cece's experience was unfortunate and discouraging. But Mack didn't lecture her or tell her what she should have done. Instead, by using a series of open-ended questions, he coached Cece to come up with the lesson herself. You can imagine how this approach must have boosted her self-confidence and her desire to keep trying.

A peer coaching session should be about discussing what the individual has been doing to practice a skill, so they can analyze what happened and what they learned from it. You can learn more about guiding someone to learn from their experiences in Chapter 6 of *Connect with Your Team*.

You can tell from these examples that a lot of coaching is just helping people pick themselves up from mistakes and failures and getting back on track. One of the most helpful things you can do in situations like this is to offer feedback that encourages. How to do this effectively is the topic of the next chapter.

FEEDBACK
That Feels Good

Feedback isn't criticism. The best feedback
addresses behavior in a way that builds a
person up.

Not every peer coach has the advantage of observing the person they're coaching. If you don't have first-hand knowledge of how a person goes about their work, it wouldn't be appropriate for you to give them feedback. Leave that to the people who interact with them often. On the other hand, you *can* give effective feedback to coworkers you do observe regularly. In that case, this chapter will be helpful; so read on!

There's a big difference between criticism and feedback. Criticism is an expression of displeasure. Criticism happens when someone is so put off with what a person has done that they let their anger take over and verbally attack them. I'm talking about things like put-downs, name-calling, and sarcasm. The assault could be disguised as a toxic question, such as "What's the matter with you?" or "Why did you do that?" Criticism is always negative and mean-spirited.

But letting a person know when their behavior is causing problems can be very helpful. The key is to hold a mirror up to a person's behavior in a way that builds them up, rather than tears them down.

There are three easy ways to do this. The first is known as "constructive feedback." The method is quite easy: *sandwich your feedback between two positives.*

Step 1: Affirm the good. You don't want to sugar-coat your feedback, but if you only mention the unwanted behavior, it will make the person think you haven't noticed the good things they've done. They'll sense you're being unfair and want to discount your feedback. To defuse defensiveness, before you give your feedback, mention at least one thing related to the actions at hand that you appreciate. For example: "Hal, most of the time you're very supportive of what people are doing."

Step 2: Describe specifically the problem behavior. To do this, you need to have observed the event first-hand. You can't rely on what others have said; if they've observed it, it's their job to give the feedback. And the description needs to be specific. For example, "Jess needed your help yesterday and you didn't make time for her."

Step 3: Explain the impact. Describe the consequences of the behavior. For example: "Jess had to stick around for an extra two hours, and she left out some critical information."

Step 4: Reset expectations. Discuss with the other person what they could have done instead. For example: "I've seen you go the extra mile for people when they've needed help. How could you have handled this differently?"

Step 5: Encourage and offer support. These positives are the other piece of the sandwich. For example: "I see you as the kind of guy who wants to have people's back if they need it. And I promise to be there for you."

Another kind of feel-good feedback is affirming something done well: praise, recognition, acknowledgement—any kind of feedback that focuses on someone's effort or achievement. Like constructive feedback, positive feedback describes specific behavior. A general comment such as "Great job!" might feel good, but if you want more of that kind of performance in the future, it helps if the person knows exactly what was appreciated. For example: "Candy, I loved your presentation. You got right to the point and gave some good examples of how the new program has benefited people."

A third kind of feedback is called "feedforward," because it doesn't focus on past behavior. Instead, it focuses on the future, mentioning specific actions that you'd like to see more of. For example: "Terry, you always have good input, and it provokes a lot of discussion. How about in our next meeting you ask some of the others about their ideas?"

As I mentioned up front in this chapter, your relationship with the person you're coaching may be such that you rarely see them in action, But if you ever have the occasion to observe behavior and give feedback, here are a few tips to make sure it builds people up:

- Keep the feedback private
- Check that the person is ready to hear it
- Make it as fresh and timely as possible
- Focus on one issue at a time
- Be honest
- Own your feedback
- If the person responds, listen to understand

Kiara holds a mirror
up to Jolene's
behavior
—in a nice way....

As Jolene's peer coach, Kiara has been helping Jolene to engage the thinking of her coworkers...

Kiara: "That meeting yesterday was pretty interesting."

Jolene: "What do you mean?"

Kiara: "I was thinking about Serena. She seemed deflated because several of the people she recruited for her test have dropped out."

Jolene: "Right. I thought she was going about it wrong. She needs to have some incentives and get signed agreements."

Kiara: "I heard you suggest that to her."

Jolene: "I did. I think that's her problem."

Kiara: "Do you remember her reaction?"

Jolene: "She didn't say much."

Kiara: "You and I have been working on your asking the kind of open-ended questions that get other people to think."

Jolene: "Yeah...."

Kiara: "It seemed to me that this was a perfect moment for you to ask her for her thoughts. But instead, you gave advice. And it didn't seem helpful."

Jolene: "Hmmm. I guess I blew it."

Kiara: "Actually, I think you've been doing really well. But nobody bats a thousand. I see this as something you can learn from."

Jolene: "I guess so. What should I learn from it?"

Kiara: "You tell me."

Jolene: "Ha! Right. I've been trying, and I'm surprised I missed that. I need to keep trying. I need to keep my radar tuned for opportunities to ask questions that get people to think."

Kiara: "I agree. With that attitude, I'm sure you'll handle it better next time."

Jolene: "Thanks, coach!"

IN SUMMARY...

Improving a skill is something we all can do, but it's a journey—a process involving many repetitions, some successful and some not. The missed opportunities and awkwardness that are par for the course can be discouraging. If as a coach you're in a position to observe the person's behavior, you may be able to give feedback that promotes learning. But it has to be the kind of feedback that uplifts.

For more about feedback, read Chapter 10 of *Connect with Your Team*. You'll learn more about encouragement—the other half of the "feedback sandwich"—in the next section.

ENCOURAGEMENT That Energizes

Even strong, capable people can get discouraged. They may be resilient, but sometimes unexpected mistakes or difficulties can take the wind out of their sails and make them doubt themselves. A series of stumbles can cause them to be so disheartened that they want to give up. They can lose sight of what's possible, feeling that continuing to strive isn't worth the effort. They "lose heart."

This is what we call *discouragement*.

If this happens to the person you're coaching, you can help them recover.

Most people have the idea that offering encouragement is a no-brainer, that if you care about someone, encouragement comes naturally. However, there's a best way to help a dispirited person.

> **It's easy to give the kind of encouragement that actually lifts a person up.**

First, appreciate that there are mistaken ways to encourage that can have the opposite effect. The classic mistake is false assurance. Has anyone ever told you that "everything is going to be all right"? Even though they may have offered it with a kind spirit, statements like this are empty if they have no basis.

Another way some people try to encourage is to sugarcoat reality. Someone might say, "This isn't so bad." Downplaying an unpleasant truth is common enough, but anyone who's been brought to their knees by adversity knows that denying it doesn't help.

Some people think encouragement means taking a tough love approach, and they say something like, "Come on, stuff happens. Get over it."

Discouragement happens when an adverse situation causes someone to be so focused on their pain and the negatives that they're no longer acknowledging the positives of their situation—even though the upsides are real and valid. Every situation is a mixture of negative and positive elements: challenges and opportunities; problems and solutions; advantages and disadvantages; mistakes and lessons learned.

As with any communication skill, the first step is to notice when someone is down. Your job will be to help them recover a balanced perspective—one that reminds the person you're coaching that there's both good and bad in their situation. You can use any of these elements of encouragement in any order:

- Listen with empathy to understand
- Affirm their strengths
- Restore a balanced perspective
- Offer support

What You Can Do When Someone Loses Heart

1. Listen with empathy to understand

Listening is first on this list because when you listen, you find out how discouraged the person is and what happened to cause it. Listening isn't about telling the person what they should be thinking, feeling or doing. Instead, you focus your attention, sense their feelings, listen for the meaning, and check what you hear.

It's okay if the individual starts "venting." This is a good sign. They may need to get their feelings of frustration off their chest, and they may feel relieved afterward. It may be all they need to "snap out of it."

2. Affirm their strengths

Nobody's perfect. Everyone is a unique blend of strengths and weaknesses. The idea is to affirm their strengths. When things go wrong, the person you're coaching might blame themselves. They may experience a blow to their self-esteem and self-confidence. They may temporarily lose sight of who they are and what they're capable of.

Your job is to remind them of their strengths. They will probably be focused on the failure at hand, not their past achievements; so it can help to bring up examples of where they've succeeded before in equally tough or even tougher situations.

3. Restore a balanced perspective

In addition to a negative view of themselves, a discouraged individual may also focus on the negatives in their situation—what caused their distress. To restore a balanced, realistic perspective, acknowledge the negatives; and then remind them that the situation isn't all negative. There are also advantages, potentials, opportunities, resources and other upsides. The positives are real, too.

4. Offer support

When someone has been discouraged by difficulty or failure, they may wonder if you still believe in their ability to succeed. If you sense this self-doubt, reassure them that you're still very much in their corner.

Myla gives Rick some encouragement....

On their accountability day, Myla sensed that Rick was dispirited...

Myla: "You seem down today."

Rick: "Mmm."

Myla: "What's up?"

Rick: "I've been trying to get Jordan fired up. He's capable of doing so much more. I don't think of him as being lazy. It's just that I'd like him to do more. I need him to do more."

Myla: "Okay."

Rick: "But nothing's working."

Myla: "Can you give me an example?"

Rick: "Sure. I've been trying to get him to test a new app. I've asked him three times, and he said he would, but he hasn't done anything. This is just the latest thing. I don't want to let him go, because I think he has potential. At this point, I just don't know how to deal with him."

Myla: "So you're stuck at square one."

Rick: "Right. I feel like giving up on him."

Myla: "It must be discouraging to try so hard and not get results."

Rick: "I don't know what to do."

Myla: "No wonder you're bummed out. Sorry, dude."

Rick: "Yeah."

Myla: "It must be tough when someone doesn't respond to you."

Rick: "It is. But where does that leave me?"

Myla: "Well, for starters, I bet you've found ways to fire up others on your team."

Rick: "Sure, but this guy's different."

Myla: "Rick, I see you as a creative, persistent kind of guy. I don't see you giving up on Jordan."

Rick: "I don't believe I've given up. I like Jordan. I'm just not sure what will work with this guy."

Myla: "These past several weeks you've been working on getting people to buy in to expectations. It sounds like Jordan hasn't been buying in."

Rick: "That's a good way of putting it."

Myla: "Maybe you haven't been thinking about Jordan in terms of buy-in. What can you do differently to get him to buy in?"

Rick: "Good question. I've been using Chapter 7 of the book for ideas."

Myla: "Are you thinking about going back to the book?"

Rick: "You know, I probably should do that. I haven't looked at it for a couple weeks."

Myla: "Are we still on for next Friday? Is this your goal for the week, to mine the book for more ideas to inspire Jordan to buy in? And then see if they work?"

Rick: "Exactly."

Myla: "You're one of the smartest people I know. I'm sure you'll come up with something that'll work."

Rick: "Thanks, Myla. I'm going to give this a try."

IN SUMMARY...

Rick was discouraged, but he's a self-starter and it didn't take much to re-energize him. All Myla had to do was a bit of listening, while affirming him and his situation.

Keep in mind that replacing an old habit with an effective skill can be a challenging journey. Some people handle mistakes, failures, and frustrations better than others. If you sense that the person you're coaching is feeling discouraged, you can help them get back up, dust themselves off, and keep trying. You can learn more about encouragement in Chapter 8 of *Connect with Your Team*.

At the end, Myla remembered to clarify Rick's goal for the week, which they would talk about at the next meeting.

You Can Do It!

So, can you do this—play the role of peer coach?
Of course you can!

Peer coaching is like conducting a meeting. Anybody can do it, if they remember to do a few things that move the process forward. This book focuses on six helpful things you can do as a peer coach:

- Coach the person to set specific action goals and hold them accountable

- Listen to "get the message" when the person you're coaching is trying to tell you something

- Get them to do their own thinking

- Help them learn from their on-the-job effort

- If you've observed their efforts, give helpful feedback

- Offer encouragement when needed

Now that you've read *Peer Coaching Made Simple*, keep it handy, and refer to it as you prepare for your coaching meetings. The more you work with someone who is trying to improve in a certain area, the more confident you'll become. You'll learn to use your natural gifts for relating to people to be a supportive peer coach.

One of the wonderful benefits of being a peer coach is that while you're getting better at it, you'll be helping someone get better at doing what they need to do.

Connect with Your Team

To illustrate effective peer coaching, I've referred to the book, *Connect with Your Team: Mastering the Top 10 Communication Skills*. Its purpose is to be a guide for people working on improving the way they interact with others at work.

When we were growing up, no one taught us the best ways to listen, give feedback, offer encouragement, and other key aspects of interpersonal communication. And yet, managers lead through communication, and members of teams rely on effective communication to engage each other and promote teamwork. Communication matters.

This is why people in the workplace need to improve the way they relate to each other. *Connect with Your Team* is a unique how-to instructional reference for what we've learned through the decades are the skills that matter most.

It's possible for people to successfully improve the way they connect with each other by studying the book and practicing the skills on the job. Doing this involves replacing old relationship habits with new, improved ones. With a concentrated effort, anyone can succeed; but it will take commitment, time, and persistence.

It's so much easier to make this effort if people don't have do it alone. Their chances of success are vastly improved if they have someone to hold them accountable and encourage them. While **Connect with Your Team** is an ideal guide for the person working on being a more effective leader or team member, I wrote **Peer Coaching Made Simple** for the person who agrees to be a peer coach.

If the person you're coaching is using **Connect with Your Team**, I encourage you to get your own copy and refer to it when preparing for your coaching sessions, so you appreciate what the person you're coaching is trying to work on.

By the way, I've written a similar book, **Connect with Your Kid**, for parents.

Dennis E. Coates, Ph.D.

CEO and Co-founder of Performance Support Systems

Dr. Coates has been a human resources development professional for over 35 years and CEO of Performance Support Systems since 1987.

He has created award-winning brain-based learning and development programs for leaders and teams for over 30 years, including these online coaching and reinforcement programs for building communication skills and core strengths:

- Strong for Performance—online coaching for people in the workplace

- 20/20 Insight Gold—online individual, team and organization feedback surveys

Over the years, these programs have helped millions of people grow stronger for the challenges of work and life.

For information about our tools, visit:

https://GrowStrongLeaders.com/

Today Dr. Coates spends most of his time writing about personal development, communication skills, core strengths and parenting teens.

Made in the USA
Middletown, DE
09 January 2021

31056633R00036